T0113865

MOUNTAINTOP
BREAKDOWN

A Mental Health Devotional

KELSEA TAFT

WESTBOW
PRESS®
A DIVISION OF THOMAS NELSON
& ZONDERVAN

This book is a work of non-fiction. Unless otherwise noted, the author and the publisher make no explicit guarantees as to the accuracy of the information contained in this book and in some cases, names of people and places have been altered to protect their privacy.

WestBow Press books may be ordered through booksellers or by contacting:

WestBow Press
A Division of Thomas Nelson & Zondervan
1663 Liberty Drive
Bloomington, IN 47403
www.westbowpress.com
844-714-3454

Because of the dynamic nature of the Internet, any web addresses or links contained in this book may have changed since publication and may no longer be valid. The views expressed in this work are solely those of the author and do not necessarily reflect the views of the publisher, and the publisher hereby disclaims any responsibility for them.

Any people depicted in stock imagery provided by Getty Images are models, and such images are being used for illustrative purposes only. Certain stock imagery © Getty Images.

Scripture taken from the King James Version of the Bible.

ISBN: 978-1-6642-7566-9 (sc)
ISBN: 978-1-6642-7567-6 (e)

Library of Congress Control Number: 2022915163

Print information available on the last page.

WestBow Press rev. date: 08/29/2022

Contents

Introduction

I have anxiety and obsessive-compulsive disorder (OCD). OCD is not just cleaning all the time or being a germophobe. It comes with a lot of its own anxiety and depression. I first found out I had OCD when I started college. I was having a lot of trouble with school and it was affecting my grades. I had always had trouble with getting stuck with stuff since I was probably twelve, but it never became a real issue until college. I went to my doctor, who suspected it was OCD but wanted me to follow up with a counselor who dealt with OCD. I did, and she helped me out a lot. In fact, she helped me so much that I was inspired to change my major to psychology. Maybe then I could help other people like me. Mental health is extremely important to talk about, and unfortunately, it is not talked about much in the church/religious community. I want to change that. We need to change that. We must change that. At the end of this book, I will give my testimony of how God has helped me with my mental health. I want you to read and take in these words by putting yourself in them first. Then at the end (if you have any doubts about whether God can work in your mind), I will share what glorious things He has done. The order of the thoughts in the book bounces between anxiety, depression, high places, and low places. It is not in a categorized manner. I am leaving it as such because, when you struggle with anxiety and depression, nothing is categorized. It just is, and comes as it will. You have to take the highs and the lows, and the goods with the bad. I hope that something in this resonates with you, or at least gives you a bit of insight into a topic that affects many people.

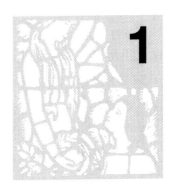

"I Must Be a Bad Christian"

YOU ARE NOT A BAD CHRISTIAN IF YOU STRUGGLE WITH anxiety or depression. Period. I am familiar with both of those. Sometimes you definitely feel like a terrible Christian when you struggle with mental health, but you are not. We need to end the stigma of mental health in the Christian community. Does God want us to live full of anxiety and depression? No, but neither does He want us to live with diabetes and broken bones. It is the nature of a sin-cursed and fallen world. Let's talk about it and not be silent about this topic. Of course, we need to pray and read the Bible, because God does help us through the tough times and can even heal. However, God has blessed us with resources like doctors, therapists, and, yes, even medicine if needed. Do not be ashamed to use the resources He has given. End the tradition of not talking about mental health issues and brushing them off as a result of not praying hard enough or reading your Bible long enough. As a disclaimer, I 100 percent believe God can heal and help with mental health. He has helped me greatly! I also believe that I have to take initiative and use the God-given resources to educate myself and better help myself as well. Thank God I am in a place I can have access to those resources. I hope to help others, especially Christians, find resources and education on these topics.

"I'm Just Not Happy"

2

BEING HAPPY EVERY DAY IS HARD WORK. SOMETIMES you think you are wearing a mask to cover up the fact that you don't feel anything. I know what it's like to not be happy, so I like to make other people feel happy. If you are in a place where you aren't feeling anything, it's okay. Eventually, you will feel something again. It's also okay to ask for help and to talk about the place you are in emotionally. I'm bad about asking for help, but I'm learning to be better about it. There are many people who say they are "too blessed to be stressed" or that "Christians should always be happy and joyful." However, you can be blessed and joyful without necessarily feeling the way people think happiness is supposed to feel. I know that sounds crazy, but hear me out. I am a Christian and I definitely become stressed even when I'm blessed. I can be joyful even though I don't feel happy all the time. Depression can sometimes make you feel numb inside, but you can still be joyful in the Lord. You can recognize that He has been so good even though you may not feel happiness. If you are feeling stuck and tired because being happy is hard work, you aren't alone. You and Jesus have this!

3

"I've Been Like This Too Long"

No matter how far you have traveled
in the wrong direction, you can always
turn around.

—Unknown

WHEN YOU HAVE OCD, ANXIETY, DEPRESSION, OR
other mental health issues, it's easy to start heading
in a negative direction in your life. Sometimes that
direction can include addiction. Drugs, alcohol, video
games, shopping, bad music, social media, or other
things can become addictions. They become our coping
mechanisms or distractions from what's going on in our
minds. Unfortunately, these are often (or often become)
unhealthy coping mechanisms. One of the hardest
things about breaking free from addictions is that
breaking free can have two parts: physical withdrawals
and mental withdrawals. The physical withdrawals don't

last as long as the mental ones, but can be excruciating. However, mental withdrawals are often what cause people to relapse. If you are dealing with unhealthy coping mechanisms, you *can* turn around. It's never too late to turn around. Get an accountability partner, get into church, and dig for the positive to get you through. Fill that void with God, and He will help you turn even the biggest thing around. I've seen it and experienced it. It's amazing what God will do!

"I Am a Broken Mistake"

I KNOW THAT A LOT OF TIMES IN CHURCH WE HAVE heard this verse: "For God hath not given us the spirit of fear; but of power, and of love, and of a sound mind" (2 Timothy 1:7). Many times, I have thought when I heard that verse, *Oh, I must be broken—a mistake— because I do have anxiety, and my mind doesn't seem sound some days.* But I'm not broken or a mistake, and you are not broken or a mistake either. God doesn't make mistakes. Some of the most famous people God used in the Bible struggled with anxiety, fear, doubt, and depression. I could give more examples than would fit in this book. The next time you are struggling and can't seem to find a verse to hang on to, try Isaiah 41:10: "Fear thou not; for I am with thee: be not dismayed; for I am thy God: I will strengthen thee; yea, I will help thee; yea, I will uphold thee with the right hand of my righteousness." When you doubt everything around you, He is right there by your side, holding you up. Even if you don't feel Him, He has got you.

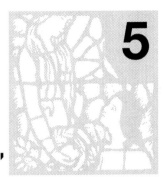

"I Am All Alone"

IT IS SO EASY TO FEEL ABSOLUTELY LOST IN THIS CRAZY world. You can be swept up with work and life and feel like you don't even know who you are any more. You feel like you are all alone in a desert that never ends. Let me introduce you to my all-time favorite verse. My best friend shared this with me when I needed it most: "Behold, I have graven thee upon the palms of my hands; thy walls are continually before me" (Isaiah 49:16). God hasn't forgotten me, and He certainly knows exactly who I am. He thinks so much of me that He engraved my name into both of his hands. He did not just write it with a ballpoint pen that will wash off with some soap and water. Nope! He engraved it. It will *never* come off. It is permanently tattooed there for eternity. That's the only identity I need to worry about. He knows my name and who I am. I know Him and as long as I have that marker in my life, I will be just fine. I am known and not alone.

"I Can't Do Anything"

THERE WERE MANY PEOPLE IN THE BIBLE WHO STRUGGLED with anxiety and being unsure of themselves. Moses was one of those. When God first called him from the burning bush, he was like, "I can't do this. I stutter, I can't speak in front of people. You would be better to send someone else." Moses was scared, so God gave him some help in the form of his brother, Aaron. For the majority of the first part of Moses's ministry, his brother did most of the speaking and crowd work for him. God will always give us the help we need until we are strong enough to find our voices. Now some will use Isaiah 26:3 ("Thou wilt keep him in perfect peace, whose mind is stayed on thee: because he trusteth in thee") to say that we are supposed to be anxiety free and not unsure of ourselves. However, that verse is talking about the peace of God which passeth all understanding (Philippians 4:7). That peace means that even *while* I am anxious and unsure, I know that God will work it out. I know that even *in* a trial, I can say hallelujah anyhow. When Moses was anxious, he prayed and used the help God gave him. It didn't make the anxiety go away immediately, but it let him be used through his uncertainty and insecurity. Now we see Moses not as someone who struggled, but as someone who prevailed. The struggle makes the man (or woman) of God who he or she is at the end of the journey.

"I Feel So Empty"

YOU CAN'T FILL FROM AN EMPTY CUP, AND YOU CAN'T write with an empty pen. Sometimes in life you start to become like an empty cup or pen. There is no tea in the vessel and no ink in the cartridge. No matter how much you try to help fill someone else's cup, you won't be successful until your cup is full. You can't write solutions or encouragement on someone else's heart until your heart's pen is full of ink. You have to keep a watch on your levels. It's not selfish. It's spiritual self-care. Burnout is a very real thing, so check your cup and pen. Do you need some more tea and ink? Refill your reservoir so you can be the best you that God made you to be. Only then can you truly help others in need.

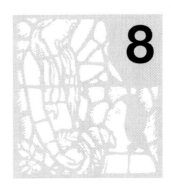

8

"I Am So Tired"

When we are tired, we are attacked by
ideas we conquered long ago.
—Friedrich Nietzsche

SOMETIMES YOU GET SO MENTALLY TIRED THAT YOU FEEL
like you are just going to break. It's not necessarily a
feeling of anxiety or even one of depression. It's a feeling
of nothingness. It is like a black hole of exhaustion. The
deepest and longest sleep will never fix this tiredness.
Even a vacation is only a temporary reprieve. So what
do you do? Well, let me tell you about clay. One of my
top five favorite books is *A Single Shard*. It is about a
young boy who works for a potter in Korea. Although
it is listed as a children's book, I recommend it for
adults as well. The setting is in ancient Korea, where
people had to collect and harvest their clay from the
river. The clay had to be malleable, which means it can

be molded, without cracking or breaking. To get it to that point, one must refine it. In the process of getting the impurities out and refining it, the potter has to do an important thing. He has to let the clay rest. Resting the clay makes it more malleable so it doesn't break or crack. The Bible says in Isaiah 64:8 that "we are the clay, and thou our potter." We, as the clay, must have a time of rest. If we do not get this rest, we risk cracking and breaking. Fortunately, our Father is the master potter. Matthew 11:28 says "Come unto me, all ye that labour and are heavy laden, and I will give you rest." I don't know what your rest will look like, but mine sometimes comes when I least expect it and in the smallest ways. Yet it is always the rest I need, and it's always right on time. I find that His rest makes me more moldable to whatever God has in the future. So if you are in the mentally tired headspace, just hold on and breathe while you wait. Your rest is coming.

9

"My Mental Health is Like Walking a Tightrope"

HAVE YOU EVER HEARD OF WALLENDA'S TIGHTROPE walk across Tallulah Gorge in north Georgia? If not, look it up, because it is pretty awesome. My granny and papa told me about it when I was younger, and now I love to stop at the overlook where he performed the famous walk. It takes some serious balance to do the walks that he did. It also takes some serious balance to have a healthy mindset. I, unfortunately, find myself with unhealthy mental imbalance quite often. If my mind were to be put into a pie chart, it would be divided as follows: mostly work, self-deprecating humor/ thoughts, coping/relaxation mechanisms (building or art videos on YouTube), and finally, church and Bible stuff. That's not balanced. When the majority of my mind is occupied with things not conducive to my mental health, the other stuff will never catch up. I love Sundays, because I know that I feel a sense of peace as soon as I step into church. Why don't I feel that all the time? It is because I am not balanced. The mind is such an important tightrope that we walk. If we fall, it isn't necessarily life or death at the moment, but the ripple effects will be felt. It can be the difference between going forward to our next destination or back to where we started.

Study Struggles

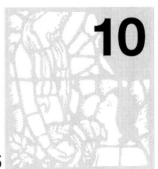

Do you become anxious about your prayer life and Bible study time? I know I get anxious about it, because it is something I struggle with a lot. There is an expectation of a certain type of prayer and Bible study that Christians are supposed to perform. However, that doesn't always work for everybody. Everyone has a different learning style and a different way that he or she expresses himself or herself. After a small get together, where the devotion topic was prayer, it was evident that prayer is a struggle for most. I think we are intimidated by the prayer format we have been taught, and feel that it is the only way to go. It is the same with Bible study and reading time. I have always felt guilty about the way I struggle with it. Then I figured something out. The way I learn and communicate does not fit the mold of traditional prayer and Bible study. I have realized that it is okay as long as I don't get frustrated and give up. What I (and anyone who is struggling with a similar problem) have to do is find out what works with my learning and communication style. For me, I found that simply getting a notebook and making a prayer journal, but using the format of writing letters, worked fantastic. In Bible study, focusing on one or two verses and meditating on those over a week's time helps me much more than trying to read a chapter or two each night.

You just have to figure out what works for you and set aside that time to spend with God. That is what really matters. You can see different styles of prayer and study throughout the Bible. David wrote psalms; Elijah prayed a short prayer and fire fell from heaven. Hannah prayed and wept on the altar. Never feel like your prayers or studies don't matter because they are different from others. Just don't give up. As you continue, your anxiety about your prayer life and study will diminish, because you will be growing closer to Him.

"I Don't Have a Clue"

Do you ever feel like the world around you has become a strange place and you are just scrambling to catch up? You act like you know what you are doing and that you belong, but your inside feels like jello in an earthquake? This is how I feel quite often. I don't have an up or a down and I am disoriented. It's one of the worst feelings ever. With all that goes on outside in the world, coupled with what's going on inside our minds, it's easy to have our internal compasses go haywire. This doesn't make you a bad person or a bad Christian. In the Bible, the early Christians experienced disorientation for sure. Maybe it was not as I described it (they didn't have jello). However, whether your disorientation comes from becoming a new Christian or dealing with the pandemic aftershocks, job changes, church issues, or big life changes, I have a few things to share.

To orient your compass, you need to find a focal point. It has to be something that doesn't change. Guess what? I know Someone! "Jesus Christ the same yesterday, and today, and forever" (Hebrews 13:8). He is Alpha and Omega. He is the beginning and the end. He has got this and He has got you! Just stick with Him and you will come through, I promise. More importantly, *He* promises.

"It's Just Hard"

> There is nothing in a caterpillar that
> tells you it's going to be a butterfly.
>   —Buckminster Fuller

SOMETIMES WRITING IS HARD. SOMEDAYS I AM DOING good if I keep one foot going in front of the other until I can go to bed at night. However, this has pushed me in a good way. It's enabled me to take a few more steps when I thought I couldn't go any further. This is because maybe someone else was having a bad day and could relate to what I was writing. Maybe they were going through what I had gone through, or will go through it at some point. Believe me, it's not all positivity, flowers, and rainbows on this side of the paper or screen. Dealing with mental illness is rough. God has helped me so incredibly much. If He hadn't, I wouldn't be here spiritually or probably physically if I am going to be honest. I still have rough spots though.

It's kind of like hiking. I love hiking in north Georgia and in the Smoky Mountains. It is my favorite thing to do. However, even before I get out of the vehicle I know there are going to be ups and downs. I also know that I am going to be tired when I get back. Somewhere in the middle, I will have to stop a few times to catch my breath because my lungs will be hurting and my bad knee will be too. When I stop, I say, "I wish we would get to a flat spot." Then, I see something interesting. It may be a frog or lizard, or a cool rock formation, and suddenly, I am ready to go. I feel the pain, but every single time I am ready to go again. I wouldn't trade those hiking moments for anything. God never promised we wouldn't have rough and painful spots, but I sure wouldn't want to go on my life's hike without Him. The wonderful thing about hikes is that the end is always amazing. To be honest, this journey of life (although exhausting), can be pretty amazing too!

"I Just Need Some Peace"

I AM ALWAYS IN SEARCH OF "PEACE." MY BRAIN BECOMES overwhelmed and I just want peace. The world's definition of peace isn't quite obtainable, however. It's an elusive thing that we try to get by buying self-help books, vacations, essential oil diffusers (although they do smell pretty good), and so on. If we are saved, we already have peace. It's not the absence of trouble, but knowing that we are going to be okay. This confidence is because we have the presence of the Almighty Savior living within us. I definitely need this reminder on a sticky note on my steering wheel, mirror, phone—basically everywhere. Why look for something elsewhere when it was with us all along?

14

Dull Mind

I HAVE A SMALL WHETSTONE THAT CAN FIT IN MY pocket. It is used to sharpen knives, hooks, or whatever you need. Our minds are kind of like blades. We have to be watchful of them and how we use them, or they will become dull and dented from the world. If I take a knife and use it in the wrong way, the blade will become dull and cracked, and it will be very hard to restore. Likewise, if I find myself using my mind in a way it's not supposed to be used, I find it affects my life, and it's hard to get back to where I'm supposed to be. If I start thinking negatively, listening to the wrong music, or watching the wrong things, my mind becomes dull and I can see the effects in my life. If I notice I am getting anxious or depressed, I have to check to see if I have started letting things in that I shouldn't. I go through my social media, music, and audiobooks to see if something is causing this dull blade. Usually there is. If I get rid of it and get my whetstones out (Bible and prayer), soon I am restored. Mental health is multifaceted and takes a bit of work, but it's worth it. The Bible says, "iron sharpeneth iron" (Proverbs 27:17). Staying around good Godly company with good attitudes will help your journey tremendously. Keep your eyes on your blade and your whetstones close.

15

"Little Is Much, If God Is in It"

SOMETIMES A LITTLE IS ENOUGH. I'M NOT A BIBLE scholar by any means, but I think a penny is roughly equivalent to one of the two coins the widow put into the treasury (Mark 12:41–44). She gave all she had, even though it was a minuscule amount to others. Sometimes you may not have a lot to give. You may be running low on your energy reserves, and the only thing you can give is just a little piece of you. That may be all you have at the moment. That is okay. God said that the widow gave more with her two pennies than the complete amount in the treasury. She gave what she had, and gave it her all. Always remember that little is much when God is in it.

16

"I Am Such a Weakling"

STAN LEE (THE CREATOR OF THE MARVEL SUPERHERO universe) once said, "Achilles, without his heel, you wouldn't even know his name today." Achilles was a strong man of legendary status, but without his weakness (his heel), he would be lost in the numerous other myths and legends of that day. It was his weakness that made him famous. He fought despite the weakness. He knew he could hide away, but he battled thousands of enemies. Once in an interview, I got the obligatory question, "What is your greatest weakness?" I gave my answer, and then they followed up with a question I had never heard before: "How would you turn that into a strength?" I didn't have much time to think about it before I gave my answer, but I have thought about it since that moment. We all have weaknesses. Sometimes it can be dealing with anxiety, depression, or other mental health issues. However, we shouldn't label it as a weakness. What if that weakness is what makes us strong? What if our weakness is what makes people see us and think, *She is a fighter.* Maybe, because of our weaknesses, they see us as compassionate, empathetic, strong, or creative. What if our Achilles' heels are what make us great in the end? As Christians, we have an advantage that Achilles didn't. Achilles died because someone targeted his weakness when he wasn't looking. He left his heel (his weakness) unprotected. However, we have the armor of God to protect us. With His armor, there is no limit to what we can do. Our weaknesses no longer define us as weak. They become the stepping stones to our greatest strength.

"Life Is a Struggle"

RECENTLY, I WAS WATCHING OLD DOCUMENTARIES, AND part of one documentary was about monks in France growing grapes. The monks knew that grapes from certain areas and fields tasted better. To discover why the grapes were so much better, the monks built walls around these vineyards and began to take meticulous notes about the land and everything they did to it. However, it wasn't until much later that the truth was discovered. The secret of the amazing grapes was stress. The grapes, when grown in soil that was depleted in some nutrients, developed more complex flavors. A vine that struggled produced more structure. On the other hand, if you have too much stress on the vine, it will fail. The monks protected the vines, making sure the vines received the right amount of stress. Stress was necessary to produce a grape which changed history and the landscape of France. The Bible says that Jesus is the vine and we are the branches. If we abide in him, the fruit will come. We may have some stress, but if we look through the leaves we will see a wall that He has built protecting us from whatever may come against us. There are so many illustrations in the Bible about God being a shelter, a wall, a protection around us. However, illustrations also abound of Him being a farmer, vine, shepherd, and living water. Yes, we may be growing in stressful soil, but look what kind of fruit we will produce. We have the best protector and vineyard caretaker of all.

"Security? Security!"

> Where does your security lie? Is God your refuge, your hiding place, your stronghold, your shepherd, your counselor, your friend, your redeemer, your saviour, your guide? If He is, you don't need to search any further for security.
>
> —Elisabeth Elliot

WE TEND TO OBSESSIVELY HUNT FOR SECURITY. WE search for financial security, emotional security, physical security, and more. Humans need security and reassurance. Companies make millions and billions by selling us a false sense of security. I have good news though! If your safe place is in the arms of a God who is everywhere, and your identity is in One who created you in His perfect image, then you can rest peacefully. You have the beautiful knowledge that you are safe, secure, and fearfully and wonderfully made.

Someone Else's Victory

THERE IS VICTORY, BUT I ALWAYS THOUGHT IT WAS FOR other people. I decided that I would just resign myself to a life of being happy for others or praying for others as they obtained victory. However, victory is for everyone. It doesn't matter what battle you are facing, whether it is mental or physical. You can have victory, and you can have hope. If you feel like you are at rock bottom and in the darkest place in your life, just lift up your eyes. There is a hand reaching down and a voice saying, "I love you." God's grace, mercy, forgiveness, and healing knows no bounds. There is hope. You can have life. You can have victory. I am so glad I can sing of my own victory now, and so I know that it is possible. It takes some work, and some days you might think it's so far away. However, the King is working alongside you, and His yoke is easy and His burden is light. Lift up your eyes because this victory is for you.

20

"God's Not With Me"

> Whither shall I go from thy spirit? Or
> whither shall I flee from thy presence? If
> I ascend up into heaven, thou art there:
> if I make my bed in hell, behold thou art
> there. If I take the wings of the morning,
> and dwell in the uttermost parts of the
> sea; even there shall thy hand lead me,
> and thy right hand shall hold me.
>
> —Psalm 139:7–10

NO MATTER WHERE YOU ARE IN LIFE, GOD WILL ALWAYS be there. If you have been running from Him, He will be there. If you are walking through a dark place in life, He is there. I've run from Him in the past and I've walked through many dark places. No matter what, He was there. I am so thankful that we have a God who never lets us go. Whatever you are battling or facing, just take a look around; you will see that you are not alone and have never been alone. He never fails us, even though we may fail Him. God is so great! His grace and mercy will always be right there, never ending and forever healing.

Foggy Mountain Breakdown

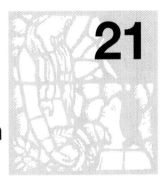

21

D<small>O YOU EVER GET LOST IN AN OCEAN OF MENTAL FOG?</small> I do. Things will be going fantastic, and I'll be on top of the world. Then, it's like a wall of fog slams into me like a ton of bricks, and I'm brought low. But do you know what? I never left the high place. I just could no longer see how far I had come at the moment. As soon as the fog lifts, I am always able to see again. I just have to be still and wait for the weather to change. Just because it's a bit foggy doesn't mean you're in the valley. It means you are high enough to be among the clouds. The views are great when you're resting in the arms of Jesus, with or without the fog. "Be still, and know that I am God" (Psalm 46:10).

Reset and Redo

SOMETIMES, WHEN RELYING ON GOD, ONE HAS TO START over every minute, or every second. Some days, it's easy to rely on God. That's when everything is going smoothly. However, when life gets bumpy, I have to step back, take a moment, and tell myself that I am going to start over. The great thing about starting over is you don't have to wait a certain period of time to start over. You can start over at any point you need to. It can be in the morning, afternoon, or at night. If you find yourself not trusting or relying on God, just take a deep breath and know He has got this, and He has got you.

Low Power Mode

IT SEEMS THAT WE ARE CONSTANTLY RECHARGING AND restoring the power in our devices. We recharge our devices multiple times throughout the day. However, in our busy lives, we forget about our spiritual batteries. We battle anxiety, depression, stress, and more, and it wears us down little by little. We forget that we need to recharge. Sometimes we neglect ourselves so much that we go into low power mode or, unfortunately, we spiritually go dead. I have good news though! We have a lifeline and the ultimate restoration. Jeremiah 30:17 says, "For I will restore health unto thee, and I will heal thee of thy wounds, saith the LORD." The well-known twenty-third psalm says, "He restores my soul." We must keep track of our energy status; if we start getting low, we should plug back in to the One who is the ultimate restorer. Be gentle with yourself and realize that you do need to be recharged. (We aren't a certain funny bunny battery mascot.) God is more than happy to help us out. He will pour out the spiritual power we so desperately need.

24

Lamb or Lions

> I am not afraid of an army of lions led by
> a sheep; I am afraid of an army of sheep
> led by a lion.
>
> —Alexander the Great

SOMETIMES WE HEAR A LOT OF INSULTS ABOUT OUR FAITH.
We are just a bunch of sheep being led to the slaughter.
We are tied down by our religion and are too dumb to see
the "truth." People who speak this way talk big and think
they are "lions." In reality, they are just lost. Psalm 23 talks
about our Shepherd who guides us through valleys and
makes sure we are fed. But our shepherd is also the Lion.
He is the great Lion, the Lion of Judah, and if we follow
Him, we will conquer. The valleys will be exalted, the hills
made low, and the crooked path made straight. Anxiety
has to bow a knee at the name of the Lion, and depression
cannot stay in His presence. We may be sheep, but we are
sheep led by the Lion. He will always lead us in victory.

"I Need a Fire"

For I, saith the Lord, will be unto her a
wall of fire round about, and will be the
glory in the midst of her.

—Zechariah 2:5

Fire. It keeps the darkness away in the night and
is a place of community during the day. No creature
of the dark will risk coming close to the fire. Anxiety
and depression will cause our minds to think the
darkness is going to swallow our light, and we feel
the oppressive nature of the darkness closing in. But
hold on just a little longer. God will build a fire. It
will be a wall of fire that nothing can get through,
and it will protect us who are covered by the blood.
Inside of this wall we can be at peace, surrounded by
the glory (fire) of God, while knowing that He has
wrapped us up in His arms. We may hear the snarls

of the creatures of the night, but we can rest assured they can't even touch the fire, much less get through it. It may seem scary right now, but trust His fire. It has never failed and never will.

Testimony

I am a pastor's kid. I've always been an anxious person. The first panic attack I can remember was at church, and I was still small enough to be playing around the benches. The preacher said something about eternity. I couldn't imagine that time concept and I had a panic attack. I didn't know it was a panic attack then but, as a child, I thought I was dying and I was so terrified. Thus began the journey of my anxious life. I had panic attacks on and off throughout childhood, and still have them occasionally. I remember vividly the summer when I was twelve and I started being bullied because I was different. I didn't think I was different. The bullying made my anxiety worse and soon introduced me to a new "friend": depression.

Around the age of seventeen or eighteen, I experienced what is commonly known as "church hurt." I won't go into it, but my family was hurt. I was angry and couldn't do anything to help them. With my anxiety, depression, and now anger, I was spiraling. I remember staying up all night so many times in what I would call a manic state of panic. Most of the time, I would not even know what I was panicking over. I would get so depressed, that I didn't even want to live anymore, because I thought there was no point. I was on an up and down roller coaster and I just wanted to get off. When you are bullied and then hurt by people who you trust (or should be able to trust), you get into a bad place. I hated myself and everybody. On top of having massive panic attacks and depression bouts, I thought that if what I saw in people was Christianity, I didn't want it. So I gave up on it. I lost my foundation, which rocked my world and my mind even more.

At some point, you want to try anything to make the chaos in your mind and heart stop. Throughout college, I made friends that I shouldn't have and got into things that I shouldn't have. I had people in my life who enhanced the negative and offered "solutions" that seemed to work. However, when the solutions wore off, there was just more turmoil. In my mid-twenties, it caught up with me. I was doing things that were affecting my health and I hit rock bottom.

Fortunately, rock bottom is a good place to get acquainted with the Rock of Ages. God showed me His loving grace. What I had as merely "head" knowledge of a Christian walk before became a genuine "heart" knowledge. He lifted me up and gave me a new life. It is as if I am living in a life much more real than I ever knew existed. My mental health has been so much better since I turned my life over to Him. I still have rough days, but I know the One who holds me also holds my tomorrow. I can trust Him. Sometimes I need a gentle reminder, but the Holy Spirit never fails to come by. Sometimes it is through a song or maybe some random occurrence. But He always says, "Rest. I have got this." I can never thank Him enough for what He has done. I want to help others who may have gone through or may be going through mental struggles. I've been there, I know how it feels, but I do know there is hope. It is Hope that endures whatever may come.

Printed in the United States
by Baker & Taylor Publisher Services